Eyes Of Evil

Shakeita Cothran

Acknowledgment

I want to acknowledge individuals who assisted with the book. I thank God for offering me diligence, insight, and inspiration for producing this book. His existence is vital for the practicality of all things. I thank my family and friends' unconditional encouragement and assistance. They provided steady encouragement and maintained optimism in my abilities, even amid self-doubt. I am still waiting for a gift that surpasses these qualities.

My friend and mentor, Mark Alexander, deserves a special thank you. Alongside his imagination competence, he also has kindness and generosity. He urged me to keep going despite the difficulties and setbacks by sharing his thoughts, ideas, and perspectives.

I express my gratitude to the esteemed reader for choosing this novel. You will find it intellectually stimulating, interesting, and motivational. I appreciate the use of your time and attention, and I appreciate your insights.

While I obtained much pleasure from authoring this book, I anticipate you will get the same fulfillment from reading its contents. I appreciate your interest and contribution.

About the Author

Shakeita Cothran is a law enforcement officer and first-time author. With over a decade of professional experience in this specific sector, she has seen several real-life incidences that functioned as compelling causes for the publication of this book. The novel has non-fiction and fiction elements, drawing inspiration from her imagination and personal experiences.

The intriguing narrative of the book delves into the more sinister facets of human nature, examining the results of our decisions and evaluating the potential for restitution.

Though she had always gained pleasure from reading and writing, it was not until she had an opportunity to establish a strong friendship with videographer Mark Alexander that the prospect of publishing a book ever penetrated the realm of plausibility. He guided her in generating ideas and inspired her to follow her passion. He also collaborated on the novel's YouTube trailer.

Contents

ACKNOWLEDGMENT I

ABOUT THE AUTHOR II

CHAPTER 1: THE GETAWAY 1

CHAPTER 2: HONEYCOMB HIDEOUT 13

CHAPTER 3: PERFECT TIMING 20

CHAPTER 4: SMALL WORLD 27

CHAPTER 5: WATCH YOUR PLUG 36

CHAPTER 6: CAN'T GET RIGHT 46

CHAPTER 7: "KEY EVIDENCE" 54

CHAPTER 8 "THE TRANSPORT" 64

CHAPTER 9: EARLY BIRD GETS THE WORM 72

CHAPTER 10: THE INVESTIGATION 77

CHAPTER 11: MISSION IMPOSSIBLE 84

CHAPTER 12: MAN AT LARGE 90

Chapter 1: The Getaway

Eastside of Lower Manhattan,

New York, United States

11:00 PM.

Television turned on...

Breaking News

"We are here, at this hour, to tell you about the unusual activities going around in the city of lights, New York," famous newscaster of CNN, Melissa James, said enthusiastically in a loud voice as she placed her hands on the table.

Watching the news, the Spanish immigrant lady in her late forties turned up the volume as she sipped on her cup of coffee.

"A small gang, comprising of three males, has caused a lot of riots in the New York city. They are convicted of major robberies throughout Manhattan. We have the Head of NYPD with us. He will be sharing further details. Stay with us." Melissa James then turned to face someone sitting beside her. At the same time camera focuses on both of them. *"Can you please share the details with us, Commissioner?"*

The Head of the New York Police Department, Adams Miller, said, *"Yes, thank you for having me. I believe you can see sketches of three suspects on the screen by now—"* The sketches appeared on the screen as the commissioner said it *"—They are the prime suspects of this case. These suspects are not adults. You might not even recognize them. They might be among you while you are sitting at a bar, drinking as casually as one can."*

"So, sir, with all due respect...why did this matter get out of hand? We all believe that NYPD is the best when it comes to cracking cases. Then, why not this one? Why do YOU have to come, at this hour in the night, to tell the people about this? Is this something really serious? Or maybe, dangerous?" Melissa James curled her eyebrows, questioning and taunting the commissioner simultaneously.

"Miss, we have no problem with solving this case. And you are right that NYPD is the best... they really are, and I'm proud of them. However, we wanted to keep our citizens aware. We have inspected every case and have concluded that they use laughing gas to knock their victims out. No physical violence.

As of now, seven house theft, including one bank robbery, has been reported. All victims, except for one lucky bird, reported that they fell unconscious when they inhaled the white gas. And what happened after, they have no slightest idea about it—except for knowing they got robbed. It is all thanks to that lady. Through her, we got their physical appearance description and other minute details that we cannot share here." He lied. There was no other information regarding the suspects. There was no eyewitness. While getting away, after robbing the house, a lady police officer saw them.

Nothing besides this.

The houses had been broken into and had no surveillance system at all except for that bank, which could not function without a security system. But these lads – they were surely clever. They refrained from talking during the robbery. They knew the advanced technology used by the New York Police Department. Their voices can be their major lead, so they only communicated with their eyes.

"Our main focus is to keep our citizens aware as either one of these prime suspects can be in their circle." The commissioner exhaled a noisy sigh and looked at the camera, *"Moreover, we just want your cooperation and, most importantly, have faith in us…wherever you find someone matching the description as it appears on the screen. Do Not. Hesitate to call the 911 dispatcher team—"* He then shot a glance at the newscaster *"—This would be all. Further details can be shared by my secretary. If needed."*

The female newscaster shifted her position from the commissioner to look at the camera. *"You heard him, folks, don't forget to call 911. Do it as if your life depends on it. Thank you. Have a nice weekend. And don't forget to watch out for yourself—"* Television turned off...

The woman got up to wash the cup she had been sipping coffee from in the kitchen. She turned on the tap water. Placing the cup under the running water, the woman sighed, *"Que dios nos ayude,"* and stared outside the glass window just in front of her, admiring the twinkling stars.

From there, she could easily see the opposite side of her house.

The Friday night was unusually brighter. Nights are not made to be bright. Moon is not made to lighten up the whole sky—little is fine. Stars were covering the sky—no signs of clouds. Nowhere to be found. Perhaps, this was the reason behind the bright night.

She was looking at her neighbor's house. They were a bunch of shady bachelors. Women were coming to their place the whole time, partying hard. That woman never liked them. She resented them for being so noisy and mannerless. Well, what else should she expect from a bachelor with no job?

Her neighbors were not home as it seemed. No light could be seen coming out of the windows. *"Ellas estan fuera, tal ve."* The woman dried the cup with a piece of cotton cloth and hung it on the cup stand. The water kept flowing.

She then shifted to turn the tap off. As she did that while peeking outside the window, she saw a car parked on the roadside of her neighbor's house. It was a Honda CR-V—an SUV. She realized it wasn't their car—her noisy neighbor had a 2001 Dodge Ram. But she couldn't care less and ignored it. There was nothing to be aware of.

However, she kept looking at the scene. Her eyes did not avert from the car; she was curious.

Three masked people stepped out of the car. One of them, wearing a crooked man mask, came out for a second or two, then went back to settle himself on the driving seat. He took out the microphone and placed the earpiece in its designated position. The woman could see his lips moving.

The other two males—the cloth masked and Joker's masked—walked towards her neighbor's door. She still had no clue what was happening. But then, something suddenly dawned on her. The men perfectly fit the description as shown in the news.

Not that she liked her neighbors; however, she was a responsible citizen. And she felt the need to inform the police about it. She already suspected her neighbor of being involved in indecent activities. It could be part of their game. Or they might've messed with the wrong people.

Whatever it was. It wasn't something that fits to be taken lightly. Without wasting another moment, she rushed to her living room, picked up her phone, and dialed 911.

Ringing...

Line connected!

"911 Dispatcher. What is your emergency?" a male representative of the 911 dispatcher said to the Spanish woman on the other side of the phone.

"Señor! I saw some masked men breaking into my neighbor's house." The woman whispered into the phone speaker as she pressed it against her mouth.

"Ma'am, can you please repeat it again? We lost you for a second."

"Sir! There are some suspicious men in my neighborhood!" The Spanish woman mumbled, breathing heavily.

"Ma'am, can you describe their appearance?"

"They fit the description of some robbers I saw on the news! They are wearing masks. One is in the car waiting outside. The other two are in the house. I just saw them!" The woman whispered as she walked towards her kitchen to peek outside. *"Are you sure, Ma'am? That they are the one?"* *"Even if they are not. Still, they are suspicious!"* The woman yelled at him.

"Okay, Ma'am. We have filed your complaint. The officer patrolling in your area will be there in five minutes."

"Please hurry! I am scared! They might come to my house!" The woman cried.

***

Meanwhile...

"JB, you there? Over." The boy wearing a black cloth mask said over the mouthpiece of the microphone. He was a juvenile.

They had this intrusion planned a week before. They knew that the boys, owners of this house, won't be there. So they took their chance to rob them. But how did they know? Cameras. They had placed the camera on their target's house door. And for the whole week, they had been watching them bring in girls, taking some interesting things inside. Since the house owners were not clean themselves, there was no harm in robbing them.

It was like a robber robbing other robbers.

The man sitting inside the car's driving seat—wearing a crooked man mask—while having a tight grip on the steering wheel and his eyes glued on the side-view mirror of the car replied in annoyance, but kept his voice low, *"Yeah, I am right here, sweet boy—"* He then rolled his eyes *"—Over!"*

In the house... The gang's leader, the man wearing Joker's mask, was standing behind the boy wearing a black cloth mask. He slapped the back of his head to get going.

"What the hell, Lil-C?" The boy mumbled.

"Toyz." Lil-C shot a deadly look at him despite the mask he was wearing. But the boy knew what his face looked like from the inside. Terrifying. And he really did not want to die by his hands, especially during their hunt.

They entered the first room on the right side of the first floor. It was a mess. It smelled so bad that the juvenile almost puked. Lil-C walked through the room and stopped near the closet. He opened the two-door closet, and with his hands, he moved all the hanging clothes to one side in one blow. His gaze from the roof of the closet moved toward the bottom. There, he saw a white box. It was a safe. He then motioned his index fingers in the safe's direction. With just a turn of his face towards Toyz, he commanded him to collect whatever was in it.

Toyz, though a juvenile, was a professional at breaking the codes. He knew how to pick on extremely difficult locks, also the safes. Imagine he opened a bank underground safe full of money. This would be no big deal for him. And it really wasn't.

"*Can you do it?*" Lil–C questioned Toyz's expertise as he folded his arms. "*Huh, piece of cake.*" He got down on his knees and placed his right ear on the safe's knob.

He closed his eyes, trying to focus on what was moving inside...the lock system. As he heard the voice—that was his target—he opened his eyes immediately. And that's how he opened the safe.

Watching him open the safe, Lil–C then pressed the mouthpiece of the microphone against his mouth. "*What's the condition, JB?*"

"*Clear for now,*" JB replied.

"*We're coming in five. Heat up the engine,*" Lil–C commanded him with his deep voice.

"*Roger that.*" JB moved his right hand down and rotated the key to start the car.

As he hit to start the car, he saw a flash of light—coming from behind—through the car's side mirror.

"*Boss. We've got a situation over here. It's the NYPD.*"

They started to stuff the things into the bag. While putting things inside their bags, they heard a police car siren.

"*Guys, guys...hurry up.*" JB's voice trembled in fear. The other two followed what he said and zipped the bag quickly. They ran downstairs to escape.

***

Knock on the door...

The neighbor who had called 911 opened the door. A woman police officer was standing right in front of the door. The male police officer, on the other hand, remained seated in the car's driving seat.

"Oh, officer! Thank God you are here. Please hurry...I think they are still in there!"

"Ma'am, can you point out which house you are talking about?"

"The one right in front of mine." The woman held out her hand and pointed her index finger toward that house.

At the same moment, she heard—them coming out of the house in a hurry—forced footsteps from the same location. It was them!

Lil-C immediately opened the car's door—with the bag in his hand. He didn't even close the door when JB hit the car on the road to escape, leaving behind Toyz—the juvenile.

"Hey! Hey!" The male police officer—sitting in the car—yelled and gunned the police car's engine.

The lady police officer, on the other hand, chased the juvenile on foot. The neighbor woman, watching all the commotion, immediately bashed her door closed.

"*Hey, Jess. You after the third one?*" The police officer said on the radio to the lady police officer, keeping his eyes fixated on their car.

"*Jess!*" He yelled as he received no response.

"*Yes, Sir. I'm on him.*" Jess was breathing heavily.

"*Where are you now?*"

"*I am on the opposite side of yours—*" Jess's voice trembled as she ran faster than before, keeping an eye on her target, "*—near the cemetery.*"

"*Got it!*" The male police officer replied. He then took out the speaker from his side and spoke on it while the police siren was on. "*Stop the car right there.*"

They did not stop. Instead, they sped the car.

On the other side...

"*Stop right there, or I'll shoot!!*" Jess shouted at him as she took out the pistol from the holster attached to her waist belt. The boy, Toyz, did not obey the order and sped up.

She was standing at the front entrance of New York Marble Cemetery—the oldest non-sectarian cemetery in New York City. Jess leaned down, placing her hands on her knees to catch her breath. As she inhaled deeply inside, she realized she had lost her target.

"*Shit!*" She cursed herself.

Suddenly, she heard the hurried footstep. She ran in its direction and saw him running towards the car. And without any further delay, she proceeded to chase after him. Toyz rushed inside the car and revved up the engine. In the meantime, Jess put her hands on the door handle.

However, he sped up the car and escaped.

Jess stood breathing heavily.

"*Jess, I lost them. Did you get him?*" A voice came from the radio. Jess shifted her mouth towards the radio on her right shoulder.

"*I lost him too.*"

"*Shit!*" The male police officer said.

She did not listen to what her partner had to say. She was distracted by the small microphone she found lying on the ground.

"*Are you there, Jess?*"

"*Yeah....yeah, I'm here. I found something. It's a microphone.*" Jess replied as she picked it up from the ground. She then wore it and heard a male's voice.

"*Toyz? You there? Toyz?*"

Chapter 2: Honeycomb Hideout

"Toyz, damn you!" JB yelled as he held the earpiece tight with one hand and placed the other on the steering wheel. His eyes turned red, and so did his face.

Thus far, they had not been chased by the police. However, his nervousness could be sensed; Lil-C could see JB's hands trembling in fear.

'I bet he got caught by the police. That dumb ass kid,' JB's mind poured in all the negative thoughts it could.

"Relax, pussy. He didn't get caught, I'm telling you. The kid's smart," Lil-C said with such confidence that it got on JB's nerves. Rather than saying anything against him, JB took out his frustration on the car's accelerator and sped up.

"Do you want to get caught too?" Lil-C said in a threatening voice. JB straightened his back and slowed down the car.

"How can you be sure he didn't get caught?"

"Just a hunch," he retorted casually.

"You and your hunches! I warned you not to take in a kid. I warned you that he would hold us back!" JB raised his voice. *"Do you know who you're talkin' to? Or should I remind you? Shut up and drive, JB."* Lil-C shot him a murderous intent. Johnny Blake, JB, couldn't utter a

single word after that. Alex Alexander, Lil-C, wasn't the man to be taken lightly. He could sense killer vibes coming from Lil-C. In half an hour, they reached their hideout. Before getting out the car, both of them removed the masks. They walked towards the door and found it unlocked.

"Did you forget to lock it?" Lil C asked as he turned to look at JB.

"No, no, I'm pretty sure I locked it."

"Follow me." Lil C rolled his eyes, pulled out the pistol from his waist, and walked inside. The hideout was unexpectedly located in a well-maintained neighborhood of lower Manhattan.

They knew notorious areas were the first ones to get searched by the police, considering that their 'offending activities' had come to the notice of the NYPD. They didn't want to take the risk of even being one of the suspects because that would ultimately lead to their arrest.

In their neighborhood, all of them had kept up with good behavior; no nightlife, no parties, no girls, and no other kind of disturbances that would end up with neighbors complaining to the police.

The three of them were living separate lives. They were all well maintained and business professionals, the last thing they wanted was the police knocking on the door. Nonetheless, they made sure to act like good Samaritan in the neighborhood. Alex was the leader; he was the one with insane physical strength though his appearance would never give an idea of him being the owner of such brute strength, and more importantly, he was the mastermind.

He was the one to decide which operation would be next. JB was the getaway driver and second in charge. However, he was involved in other activities as well when needed. On the other hand, Toyz who was a champ at cracking codes and opening the safes.

***

Alex entered the house and saw the lights turned on. He was sure he had turned them off before leaving. He changed his demeanor and became more alert as he stepped inside the living room.

Their house was designed after the honeycomb. Walls were painted in yellow and black color; the base was yellow, and the wavy stripes were black. The rooms of the hideout were hexagonal, like a mass of hexagonal prismatic cells built by the honeybees.

Their alliance was an impeccable one. All three of them were experts in their domains. This was why, until now, all of their burglary, stealing, or robbing attempts were successful.

"*It's you!*" Alex said in surprise.

"*Fuck you, kid!*" JB yelled.

"Aww, were you worried about me?" Toyz teased him. *"It's not funny. And why the hell did you leave the door unlocked? Have you finally lost your mind? Why were you not answering me over this fuckin—"* JB took out the Bluetooth earpiece from his pocket and threw it at him *"—thing that you drilled us about!"*

Toyz impulsively caught the earpiece with his right hand. He was quite good at catching things. He was the catcher of the school's baseball team he was enrolled.

Meanwhile, Alex threw himself on the living room couch, taking a deep breath as he removed the fake skin from his eyes. He was done with their argument. *"Guys? Can you stop bitchin'?"* Alex requested as he closed his eyes to rest for a while.

Alex was a bachelor in his late thirties. He was 6 feet 2 inches tall. His facial features were appealing as he always attracted women wherever he went, whether in bars or parks. He was quite popular due to his attractive looks. Before going out on the mission, he used to wear fake skin on his face so that no one could recognize him, which almost always turned out well for him. However, his appearance was nothing more than a beautiful lie. From the inside, he was purely evil. He could extract the soul of his opponent with just one glance. When back to routine, he acted as normal as others.

"*Wait a damn minute!*" The juvenile said in shock as he jumped out of his place.

"*What the hell —*"

Lil-C's moment of silence was interrupted by Toyz due to sudden dawning on him. "*Where is my earpiece?!*" Toyz's eyes widened as if they would burst out of their sockets.

"*How the hell are we supposed to know?*" JB yelled.

"*Dumbasses, calm down! What's the deal?*" Lil-C asked, "*Was it important?*"

"*No, but what if—*" Toyz's eyes widened further; this time, his eyeballs were surely going to pop out.

"*What if?*" JB repeated.

Toyz could feel a knot tied in his throat. He wasn't able to let the words out of his mouth. Fear had taken over his body. "*What if they get it?*" Toyz said, forcing his voice out of his mouth. Whatever the case was or how many burglaries he had taken part in, Toyz was still a child. And this was the first-time police chased them, which freaked him out. They hadn't realized, but there was room for them to mess things up.

Or perhaps, room for Toyz to mess up.

"*Will they be able to trace the one you are holding in your hand?*" Lil-C asked. JB sat on the sofa with his head buried in his hands.

"We are done," JB whined.

None of the other two paid him any mind.

"I know nothing about the tracing man. But what if they do?"

"Okay, okay, calm down. Nothing will happen. I have a friend, I'll ask him about locating through this earpiece," Lil-C calmed him down. *"For now, let's see what we got. Bring in the bags."*

Within a few minutes, JB brought two bags from the car. Lil-C watched him walk inside the room as he sipped black coffee from the mug with an animated picture of a moneybag. He put aside the mug and extended his arm as JB motioned one bag in his direction. Toyz sat there in silence and waited for them to open the bags. He wasn't curious to know what was inside it. However, he remembered which items he had stuffed it with.

Lil-C rolled the zip open and exposed what was inside. *"Served 'em right,"* he smirked. The bag was full of cash. *"Open the other one."*

This one was filled with jewelry that was worth a couple grand. The gleaming jewelry reflected in their eyes; they were shining radiantly like a star.

"So, who's our next target?" JB asked.

"Oh, someone's being greedy here," Toyz teased him again.

"*Shut up!*"

"*On New Year's Eve at Greenwich, we will work on it, but for now, act normal!*" he suggested as he asked them to be cautious of their next move, "*We don't want people in our circle to get suspicious of us.*"

"*What about all the posters they have posted of us?*" JB chimed in.

"*Those bastards will never trace us with those shitty posters if we never show them ourselves,*" Toyz added as he took out the fake skin from his pocket.

"*Yeah,*" Lil C smirked. "*Let them celebrate what they have achieved. They will never get their hands on us,*" he said sternly.

30 days and 30 nights to their spree...

Chapter 3: Perfect Timing

After a hectic workday, Jess pulled over to a gas station. She intended to refill the car tank before returning home, as it had become a part of her routine. Jess stood by the fuel dispenser, and as she filled her car with gas, she looked around. She had been serving as a cop for at least a decade and had become quite observant.

A matte black Porsche car entered the pump vicinity swiftly. As its tires fractioned against the road, it caught Jess's attention. She turned her head and saw a car parked on the left, and a tall, 6 feet 4 inches, a brown-skinned male exited the vehicle. He appeared nice, wearing a grey Tom Ford suit, and gave off an expensive look. As the man walked into the gas station, his boss's attitude intrigued Jess even more.

"Oh my! How can anyone look this handsome?" Jess thought with her gaze following the handsome hunk.

His charming look appealed to Jess at first sight. She was lost until the fuel dispenser clicked, and she returned to the real world. She quickly pulled out the gas pump and hung it on the machine. The tank was full, and she was supposed to head out, yet she did not. Her eyes chased the man through the glass window.

You can't miss out on him, Jess! Her mind snapped. She had the urge to have a second glimpse of that fine piece of a specimen, so she walked into the gas station and pretended to grab a drink. Jess moved past the guy, who was now standing before the wall chiller, looking into his hazel eyes. It was all about his colored eyes and a teardrop tattoo on his face that made it even harder for Jess to look away.

****

The man had pulled the car to the gas station purposely. He felt like a car was following him. *If I am right, this car will stop by and come behind, and if not, then I will at least feel safer,* he thought, deciding to mark a stop at a gas station.

He remained conscious and kept observing what was happening outside. Meanwhile, he grabbed a drink and proceeded to the counter. Nothing serious occurred until then. He put his phone on the counter and waited for the bill.

A few minutes later, another car parked at speed in the gas station. It stopped just behind the Porsche, and someone emerged. The guy behind the counter noticed this new entry but continued billing. It was normal for him as several customers came and went by every day. However, as the new guy walked from a distance, he seemed suspicious. The station owner narrowed his eyes to look closer, and for his shock, he captured an image of a masked man with a pistol in hand. *"Get down, get down!"* he shouted and alerted everyone. No one could make an immediate sense of what was happening. The tall man followed his gaze and watched outside only to find out that very car he suspected.

Damn! That's an SUV.

He had recognized the car's model – a black SUV. But before he could utter anything, the sound of a fire roared inside the store. He quickly pulled Jess, and the two got down on the floor, moving behind the counter beside the station owner.

Everything happened instantly, and as soon as Jess realized the situation, she immediately got into her cop instinct.

The masked man continued firing at the station. As the bullets pierced the glass wall, they did not hit anyone as all three of them – the owner, the tall guy, and Jess – were on their knees. They all lay down on the floor and hid behind the counter cabin, where bullets could not reach easily.

With every second, the situation got tense. None of them knew what was happening. Unsettling thoughts rattled their headspace.

The shooting stopped soon. The gas station went into complete silence. Jess carefully peeked from a slight linear opening at the right side of the counter. She could see the man getting back into the SUV, *"He is driving away,"* she remarked. The tall guy quickly got up and rushed to get the tag information. As they raced on the road, he jumped inside his Porsche, and accelerated to chase the other car. The station owner immediately called 911 and informed them about the incident.

On the other side, Jess also hurried to her vehicle. She radioed the situation to the area police station on her way. But as she reached an intersection, she had to stop. *Damn, which way to go?* she forcefully pressed her hand against the steering and cussed. Jess had just realized that she was late to chase the culprit.

After pausing momentarily in disappointment, she took a U-turn and returned to the gas station. She walked in again and found the owner in shock on his chair. He looked scared to have experienced such a commotion. Jess offered him a water bottle, *"Relax, NYPD must be reaching soon."*

After comforting him, Jess found a phone placed on the counter. *It must belong to him,* she thought and put the phone in her pocket. Two area police officials approached the gas station in the next five minutes. Jess conversed about the situation with them. The investigation followed with officials asking questions and the owner filing the report. Jess returned home, and since she was exhausted, she fell asleep as soon as she laid down in her bed.

****

The phone rang once and then twice. Jess peeked around from the corner of her eyes. The night had been long and tiring, and Jess was still sleepy.

It was 8:30 in the morning. Jess pushed herself to get out of bed. She freshened up and ate a slice of bread with butter while gulping in her coffee hurriedly. *I have to be there by 9*, she reminded herself, pulling the jacket over her shoulders.

Jess reflected herself in the dressing mirror, all set for another adventure. As she hassled to grab her keys and cell phone off the table, something vibrated in her pocket before ringing again. Jess put it in her hand and dragged it out. *"Oh! So, here it is,"* she said, glancing at the missed calls and tons of notifications appearing through the locked screen.

But what am I going to do with it? Jess wondered, unsure. She could have handover the phone as a part of evidence to the police, but she did not.

Jess shook her head to get off the thoughts and left for work. As she reached the station, she deliberately left the phone inside the car. She worked for a few hours, and as she went to her car at lunch, she heard it ringing again. Jess answered this time; surprisingly, it was him on the other side.

"Hey," the gentleman greeted softly.

"Hey, who's this?" Jess inquired.

"*It's me, Alex,*" he responded, revealing his name for the first time.

"*Who is Alex? Do I know you?*" Jess requested patiently.

"*Actually, I am the one to whom this phone belongs,*" he claimed his possession.

Before Jess asked anything further, "*I lost it last night at the gas station,*" he added.

Things then made sense. But Jess was unsure until she asked Alex to describe his appearance, and he drew it exactly as she had seen him the other night.

Oh yeah, he is that nice looking guy that I could not get my eyes off, Jess confirmed to herself.

She was thrilled to reconnect with the dashing guy. The opportunity encouraged her to reveal her identity. "*Well, I am Jess, the one you saved last night,*" she said, mentioning, "*If you remember how we fell to the floor,*"

"*Oh yeah, I do.*" He chuckled slightly without letting her notice and asked, "*How can I get my phone back now?*"

"*You can come to the gas station again and take it from me anytime,*" Jess retorted, feeling excited to see him again. "*How about meeting at a cafe near the station, so that I can have my phone, and you can thank me for saving your life?*" He offered.

What else could be better than this? Jess thought before agreeing to him, *"Sure."*

"See you there at 7:30 today," he said.

"Okay, see you soon!" She hung up and returned to work.

Chapter 4: Small World

"I did not know I would get to see this gorgeous man again," Jess thought while scanning through Alex's image in her head.

She glanced at the clock; it was 6:10 PM Her shift ended at five, but she was still working at her desk. Jess had always been a loyal worker. Rather than rushing out at exactly five, she preferred to sit back and finish her work. *"Almost done!"* She uttered as she hit the *enter* button.

Jess shut down the system, gathered her belongings and left the premises. While driving, Jess kept wondering about the handsome man. There was not anything yet, except that his appearance appealed to her at first sight, and she was to see him once more. This thought alone made her feel the butterflies in her stomach.

As she reached the house, Jess had quite an hour to rest. She brought herself some snacks from the kitchen and sat on the couch, munching them.

The news anchor kept blabbing about one thing and the other, but who cared? Jess was lost in her imaginary world. The phone went off with a text the read, *"I am on my way,"* Alex texted his number from another one. Jess realized it was time to get ready and get going. She dressed casually – wearing a black button-down shirt with sky-blue jeans and a leather jacket – in her signature style. Her nice dark brown hair rolled down her shoulders. She brushed her hair, and before moving out, she made sure Alex's phone was in her pocket.

The café was a 15-minute ride from her place. As she-drove herself to the cafe, she had mixed feelings. She was definitely enthralled by Alex's personality and wanted to know more.

***

-Alex-descended from the Porsche and walked into the cafe. He reserved a table for the two and sat there waiting for Jess. Alex had never been flirty or crazy for women. Nevertheless, he had been with different women previously, yet none at the moment. That's what invigorated him to give it a chance.

As Jess appeared, Alex recognized her immediately. She was wearing the jacket she had on last night, so as she approached him, he stood up to welcome her. They both greeted and exchanged a few words, settling themselves down to comfort.

Jess pulled the phone out her jacket, *"Here is your cellphone,"* she put it forward towards him. *"You must have missed it a lot!"*

"Of course, I did,"—Alex chuckled and leaned forward. *"Thanks for keeping it to yourself,"* he added, taking the phone from her hands.

"No problem, I just found it over the counter so I took it rather than leaving there to be lost."

"That's so kind of you," he appreciated her again.

The rest of the talk followed by recalling the happening. Jess was curious to know if Alex could catch the masked man who fired at the store last night or find out who he was since he had gone after him.

"No, I could not get my hands on that bastard." He said in disappointment, *"Wish I could. Luckily, I did note the SUV plate number,"*

"That's okay. You surely did your best." Jess commended, adding, *"I am certain police will get him soon."*

"I hope so."

In the meantime, the waitress served the order – two cappuccinos and fudge brownies. They remained silent for a while, allowing each other to have space to breathe and contemplate, even though none of them seemed to need it. Alex was as pleased by Jess's existence as she was his. He hadn't noticed her earlier because of trailing the suspicion first and then the incident, yet he was impressed now.

"By the way, thanks for saving me. I could not have been sitting here with you otherwise," Jess expressed her gratitude. *"No, no, you don't really need to. I just made an excuse to meet you,"* he smirked as if he had

begun to get interested in her. When together, things between the two began to enhance. Jess, who fell in first, did not expect Alex to put her feelings into words. *"Are you seeing anyone?"* Alex took a sip of his coffee, looking into her eyes.

"Nope, I am not," Jess replied, giving off a brief smile.

"Good for me," he murmured, and

As she could not hear it clearly, *"What did you say?"* she narrowed her eyes and raised her brows twice, "Say it again!"

"It's just I want to ask if I can take you out," Alex somehow filtered words, *"like having a lunch or dinner together."*

Despite being good-looking enough, Alex hesitated, thinking that Jess would mind it. He had no idea how his words had overwhelmed her. *"I guess we can,"* she responded after a brief pause.

The two exchanged numbers before leaving and connected at a whole new level.

***

Days and nights went by with Jess and Alex conversing on phone. They had developed a bonding, like friends, but were certainly becoming more than that. They shared their likes and dislikes and talked about almost everything their lives had.

Even though Jess admired Alex, she didn't reveal her true work to him. She rather faked that she was into real estate. It could be due to her job's nature, or maybe she had some other reason. Whatever! They both were ignorant of each other's professions. Jess remained busy chasing the culprits and solving cases while Alex was equipped with his undisclosed work. She often did not answer his calls at work, nor did he bother her much.

After around a month, Alex asked Jess out again. He had come across a fancy restaurant and wanted to take Jess there. He told her how he would love to make Jess feel exclusive and special. Jess was already intrigued by him, so she did not think much and agreed to go on an unannounced date.

The next evening, Jess was all excited and ready for the date. She wore an emerald green bodycon, with her hair curled and a necklace around her neck. Her embellished appearance turned out to be a breathtaking sight for Alex. As he reached her house and called her downstairs, he was stunned to witness this side of Jess's personality.

Sitting opposite to each other, their eyes contacted, and they grinned. *"You are looking absolutely gorgeous. I have no words, Jess."* Alex complimented her eternal grace. Jess received the praise smiling and appreciating Alex, *"Thank you! You always look handsome, whether in jeans or suits."*

"Oh really," he teased, encouraging her to speak more of him. *"Yes, in fact, I love your physique. You have such a manly body that can impress any girl like me."* Jess was now confident to say it, as they had become good friends.

"I don't care about any girl. I want to impress you!" Alex said with a flirty look.

"I am impressed, can't you see it?" Jess confessed.

Jess surveyed the expensive restaurant through her detective gaze. Alex was right; she loved the lavish décor and cool ambience. *"They won't compromise on quality,"* She thought thinking about the food as she craved.

In the meantime, Alex felt a tap on his shoulder. It was as if someone had touched him to drive his attention. With a glass still in hand, Alex turned around only to find someone familiar standing behind him. Before he could utter a word, *"What are you doing here?"* Jess jumped in.

It was her Uncle Rob. He giggled before saying, *"Hello, kid!"* coming to the table frontside.

-Alex stood up and shook his hand, *"Hi, Rob! Nice to see you."*

What? Does Alex know my uncle's name? How is it possible? Thoughts captured Jess's mind seeing how Alex and Uncle Rob knew each other. It did not make sense, yet one thing she realized was *how small the world is! We end up belonging to each other in one way or the other.*

Uncle Rob talked to Alex for a few minutes and then left the two. *"Enjoy yourselves!"* He remarked, waving goodbye to them.

As Alex sat down, Jess did not wait for a second, *"How do you know my uncle?"* Jess asked precisely, yet super curiously.

-Alex took it very lightly and responded, *"Just because he is fond of cars. He comes often to my lot for cars, as he buys a lot, you know!"*

"Oh, I see." His response elevated her curiosity, and she came up with another question. *"What do you do for living?"*

"It's not appealing to investigate your partner on a date," he chuckled, diverting the conversation off-topic.

Investigation! It clicked Jess, and she suspected herself of revealing her true profession. She quickly changed her mind and stopped herself from asking more questions, *"Oh no, it's not like that,"* she quit.

"Why would someone investigate a hot gentleman like you?" she flirted. *"A sexy officer like you, maybe."* Alex retorted, likely, and they both laughed it off. Jess pondered over Alex's connection with Uncle Rob. She

did not have any clear indicators, yet she tried connecting the dots. Meanwhile, a waitress approached the table, asking, *"What can I get for you two?"*

Her arrival interrupted Jess's thoughts. She requested a pink lemonade, not knowing it was Alex's favorite. *"Woah! I love it,"* he exclaimed and asked the waitress, *"please make it two."*

The waitress noted their drinks and jotted down the rest of the order. She then left them and returned shortly with drinks. *"Your meal will be ready in twenty. I will serve you soon,"* she said politely, serving the drinks.

"Okay, no problem," Alex replied to her with a grin. While enjoying the drinks and awaiting the meal, Jess and Alex fell into a conversation again. They talked about how they both loved travelling and shared different experiences. The fact that they had similar interests, especially the travelling craze, aided things to flow smoothly. They did not anticipate they could take what was in between them to a whole new level with this only.

Once the tempting meal was there, Alex and Jess savored themselves. They were truly lost in relishing the beautiful moments together. When the dinner was over and the night was about to end, Alex offered something exceptional while driving Jess back home.

"Since we both love travelling, would you like to go on a weekend gateway to Mexico?" Alex invited Jess to join him on the trip.

"This sounds crazy," she jumped up from her seat in excitement. *"I mean I would love to explore Mexico,"* her eyes sparked, *"But I need couple of days to think about it, I will let you know soon."*

"Sure, nothing to rush," he understood Jess's stance and assured her, *"Take your time."*

As the car stopped in front of Jess's house, Alex got out the car and walked her to the doorstep. They end the night with a passionate kiss, *"Goodnight!"*

Chapter 5: Watch Your Plug

The music playing in the car paused abruptly. The phone placed in the holder vibrated and rang loud into the speakers. The unexpected interruption startled Lil C, who was relishing a lip-sync to the *"New York State of Mind."* His gaze shifted from the front to the dashboard. With one hand on the steering, he reached for his phone with the other.

JB calling...

Why would JB call me? He thought and, for a moment, recalled if they had to talk or meet today. They hadn't, as far as he remembered. He slid the green icon and answered the call, putting the phone on speaker.

"Where were you, man? Why are you not picking up?" JB spoke in frustration as he was calling on purpose.

"I am driving, actually," Lil C replied and asked, *"why are you calling at this hour? All good?"*

"Yes, everything is under control," JB assured.

It was around quarter past seven in the evening – *not a usual time for JB's call.* This made Lil C anticipate a problem, but luckily there wasn't any. *"We need to talk,"* he said and added, *"Meet me at the spot!"* *"Gotcha,"* Lil C knew what it would be, *"will be there in 15,"* he said and ended the call.

***

At honeycomb hideout...

As Lil C reached the honeycomb hideout, he headed straight-inside. A few neighbors noted him, but they were all quite familiar with his gentlemanly appearance. They, in fact, admired his novelty, not knowing who he truly was.

Lil-C had the keys, as each of them did. But he hadn't been to the hideout as frequently like JB and Toyz. He last visited the place after the burglary they committed in the bachelor's house. And now, when it had been two months to that, he was there to plan another.

-Lil C first knocked and, rather than waiting, unlocked the door and went in. As he walked into the lounge, he called for JB. *"I'm here, JB,"*

JB was there before him. And as Lil C made himself comfortable on the couch, he saw JB coming out of the room.

"Hey. What's up?" Lil-C crossed his legs and asked.

"I've got a lick from a friend," JB responded, sitting in front. *"I knew it,"* Lil C smirked as his intuition proved to be right. *"I've got word from one of my friends that Mexican personnel had fallen out with someone, and they are going to steal all his stuff."*

-Lil C didn't say anything in response. However, his expressions somewhat revealed his dubious thoughts. He avoided concluding at this point and pondered deeply until JB interrupted. *"He is a big-time person. He has pissed somebody off... someone who knows him well and wants to take away all he has in revenge!"* JB explained.

"We can hit up the spot and retrieve all the drugs," he added.

JB attempted to satisfy Lil-C because he wanted them to go for it. He trusted the lick provider; interestingly, he was the guy the Mexican had pissed off. And that's the very reason the guy was setting him up for the robbery. The guy was also a friend of JB. He had led JB to several licks before, and since none of them went in vain, JB had a reason to put his faith in him.

JB knew on whom he was relying, and thus, he convinced Lil-C as well. They both discussed it for a while. And as Lil C had always been up for a thrill, he soon agreed.

The team of three – JB, Toyz, and Lil-C – began the homework immediately. They were to study their new target and get to know everything about him.

The guys spent the night planning. In the meantime, they kept recalling their mistakes and reminding each other what not to do this time. JB threw a paper ball to Toyz and taunted, *"Be cautious, kid. Practice running a little faster."*

"I'm at least better than you, dickhead, who can't risk running on feet, so better stick behind the wheel," Toyz responded furiously.

Lil–C interjected the conversation, *"Can you guys please just shut up and focus on work?"* He stared at Toyz and continued, *"We don't have much time to waste."*

Toyz felt as if the look of aggravation was for him only.

"What? Why are you giving this look to me only? JB started it, you know."

"Because you are the one who messes up things," Lil–C replied.

"JB is right. Don't leave anything this time," he advised.

"You guys better watch out for yourselves. I can take care of mine." Toyz was annoyed, so he left the room.

For the next couple of days, JB and Toyz surveyed the house. They cautiously explored the surroundings and learned a few necessary things about the neighbors. They observed the target's movements closely and placed a vehicle tracker to know his whereabouts all the time. To their surprise, the home had an ADT security system. And avoiding the security alarm was to become a challenge, and they knew it. So, the guys acted smart and planned accordingly. They decided to walk inside the house rather than break in, which would save them from invasion risk.

Moreover, studying the target for a week revealed much about him. They found out that the homeowner, the Mexican guy was a businessman and had a girlfriend. The consistent follow-up gave an outlook on their schedule.

With all the knowledge, the guys planned to mark Saturday for the intrusion as the two would habitually return late from a party, and it would be easier to walk them in.

***

Saturday, 2 AM...

It was dark with minimal moonlight around. The streets were dead empty, with nobody strolling by, not even the stray cats and dogs.

It appeared as if everybody in the neighborhood had also fallen asleep. This, altogether, eased the robbing challenge. JB, the getaway driver, drove the three to the target location. With their keen observation, they had figured out that the Mexican would return home by 3 or 4 late at night, so the guys showed up half an hour before. JB cleverly parked the car a few meters away from the house and turned off the engine.

It was their time to get ready. Each of the three put their masks on. They took their communication gadgets and ensured they had everything - the guns, bags, and rope. Once everything was in place, they stepped out of the car and moved towards the house quietly.

JB and Toyz followed Lil-C as he climbed up the wall. The three jumped into the backyard one by one. As per the plan, they cautiously moved behind the garage with their bodies half-bent to avoid the only security camera it had.

"Keep your head down," Lil-C pressed Toyz's head down and whispered as if it could have been recorded.

"Eh!" Toyz made a sound pushing his hand, *"Got it, man."*

Once there, they quickly took their positions. Lil-C and Toyz sat down on either side of the garage's backside. JB hid behind a large-sized dumpster, which was placed at the left corner of the garage, adjacent to the outer wall. As they hid in the backyard, they were not visible offside the wall. One could not even notice them, even if inside, as it was pretty dark there. Lil-C glanced at Toyz settling down and noticed JB still moving around. He pressed the mouthpiece and directed the two. *"Take your positions fast. Over!"* Their phones pinged slightly, and the screen displayed a movement. *"The vehicle is moving. They are on their way back,"* Toyz confirmed the commotion.

Their eyes stuck to the screen, and they followed the tracker. The three waited fifteen minutes for the couple to arrive.

When they were to approach finally, JB alerted Toyz and Lil-C, *"they are here."*

JB had a wider angle of view; he could see outside as he sat beside the external wall. *"Be ready. They are coming!"* he emphasized as their black SUV passed through his side and slowed down.

"Roger!" Toyz and Lil-C's voices emerged in unison, *"Roger that!"*

The car rolled inside the main gate and headed straight into the garage. The two hiding behind waited for the car to enter, and as soon as it did, they moved into the garage swiftly.

The man and the woman did not notice until they exited the vehicle and were upheld at gunpoint. The two seemed drunk but they complied with Lil-C's commands. *"Shut the fuck up and move!"* Lil-C touched the guy's shoulder with his pistol, demanding him to walk ahead.

With Toyz pointing at the girl and Lil-C over the man, they walked them to the main door. *"Open it up!"* Lil-C ordered the man, and as he stared back at him, Toyz interjected. *"Don't even think of doing anything,"* the kid warned him for his girl's sake.

The Mexican man did not think twice. He quickly put in the security code without any hesitation. JB, who was watching behind, also joined them. And as the door unlocked, they rushed the couple inside and shut the door behind them.

Inside the house...

Lil-C and Toyz exchanged senses. He made a gesture instructing Toyz, *"You hold her downstairs,"* while JB and I escorted-the guy upstairs to retrieve the drugs.

Toyz shoved the girl onto the couch and stood over her with a gun, waiting for the two.

On the other side...

Lil-C watched over the guy while JB went ahead to collect the drugs.

The home telephone rang...

Amidst collecting drugs upstairs, JB's attention shifted to the phone hanging on the wall. Lil-C was also cautioned. The answering service picked up the call, *"911 dispatch speaking,"* the voice declared on speaker. *"Is everything okay? Do you need us to send an officer to you?"* The first question that ran through their mind was *how did the police know to call?* And the only answer could be that one must have signaled them. Before Lil-C could process, the caller (NYPD) left the message, *"Don't worry, we have sent a unit-your way to check in!"*

Lil-C's mind automatically turned to the man, and his calmness served as evident. He appeared at peace as if he knew the cops were on their way and would show up anytime soon.

With his experience, Lil-C figured it out – the man had put in the distress code, and NYPD called to confirm it.

They must be reaching soon, his mind triggered.

Lil-C peeked at his watch and calculated the time. They had been inside for 10 minutes, and police must take at least 15 to reach there. It meant that they hardly had five minutes more to wind up.

He signaled JB, who was busy stuffing the drugs in a bag, to hurry. As soon as JB finished and got up, they rushed to the basement. JB hassled to the safe and took out all the money in just a minute.

He zipped the bag, *"done!"* and stroked Lil-C at the back, indicating, *"let's get going."* Lil-C and JB went up, joined Toyz, and rushed out of the home together. JB stepped out first, with Toyz running behind him. Lil-C ensured to lock the door and exited the house at last. The police were not visible anywhere on the road; however, they could hear the sirens wailing at a distance. This alerted them to be cautious and waste no time.

JB sat behind the wheel. He gunned the car engine while Toyz tossed the bags in first and then jumped in alongside Lil-C. The car hit the road, making the three run off and disappear in seconds.

Chapter 6: Can't Get Right

Keys rattled, and the door unlocked.

The trio had made it to the hideout. They walked inside the yellow-black den, laughing over the thrilling experience they had just had. JB threw the bags on the floor and relaxed on the couch. With his one leg resting up high, he snatched the earpiece off his ear and was in the mood to call it a night.

-Lil C, on the other hand, was thirsty. He went straight for the water, and while sipping it, he noticed JB teasing Toyz. *"Chill, man!"* he said as their eyes briefly met.

However, JB continued to credit himself. Seeing that, Toyz smirked and exchanged a mischievous look with Lil C. Even though it was JB's plan and his friend had gotten the lick, all three had been involved equally and, thus, held equal credits.

Perhaps, even though the money and drugs were twice what they had looted from the bachelors, none cared. For them, the process - the fear, the thrill, and the fun - mattered, not the money.

Lil-C patted Toyz, *"You did a great job, kid."*

"I always do," Toyz appeared in confidence, only until JB's voice cut him off, *"What good did he do except tie up the woman?"* It only took a second for Toyz's confidence to shatter into pieces. All the goodness

faded away, and his face turned pale as JB said, *"Wait, wait. I don't even remember seeing Toyz with the rope...."*

"Nor did I," Lil C agreed.

"Where's the rope, Toyz?" JB questioned.

As JB and Lil C turned to Toyz, his blank face was an answer that *he never tied the woman, nor he had the rope.*

He hammered his hand against the wall and shouted, *"Fuck, feck...,"* cussing himself.

"What the hell, man?" JB stood up in awe, while Lil-C was also in anger and disbelief.

"You dropped the earpiece last time, and now I know damn well you've left the fuckin rope." Lil C's words roared as he walked out angry.

JB followed Lil-C, *"Your only job was to tie the bitch, and you couldn't even do that, dumb ass!"*

The door slammed loud, leaving Toyz in the room all alone.

***

The following day, JB called his friend, the guy who informed them of the lick.

"Yo, what's up?"

"Nothing, just wandering as usual." He replied and asked impatiently, *"How did the party go? Did it work?"*

JB giggled, *"Yeah, it did."* He responded and revealed the purpose, *"I've called you for the very reason."*

"Come through," he added.

When the guy got there, JB first thanked him for his contribution. The group then sat together to split the profit among four – the three of themselves and the lick provider.

They altogether had robbed and had gotten six bricks (kilos) that was worth around 180 thousand dollars. When distributed equally, each of them got one-brick valued at 42 thousand dollars in cash. The reward certainly outweighed the anticipation. The source guy, JB and Lil C got their equal share. But when it came to Toyz, they came with something new.

"Toyz don't deserve even half of it," JB said.

Toyz stared at JB, thinking, 'Has he lost his mind?' His eyes then shifted from JB to Lil C and the other guy. The two also seemed in agreement with JB. And before he could argue, Lil C continued to say after JB. *"Since you fucked up the second time, you must take less."* *"That was never said before."* Toyz retaliated to JB eye to eye. *"How? Anyone could have made that mistake."* *"A mistake isn't meant to be repeated,"* JB mocked him again. Even though Toyz was never fond of acquiring more money or dying for it, the idea of giving him less just because he made an error pissed him off. He could see the group turning against him collectively, so he stood on his behalf. *"It was not decided before, nor it's justified now,"* He pronounced.

Toyz argued that what they said wasn't fair, and he would never agree with those terms. The debate soon heated and led Toyz to an extent where he drew up his hands and yelled out, *"I'm done with this shit. I'm out!"*

***

A week passed by...

'It's time to sell now,' Lil C thought as his fingers dialed.

He called Jess's uncle, the popular dealer, Rob. They both had a good business relationship, not limited to trade only since Jess had introduced Rob as her uncle to Alex. He had often contacted Rob, and this time was no different as he was going to discuss a deal. And since it had always profited Rob, he was never interested in finding who Alex worked with or how they had their hands on dope every couple of months.

As Rob answered the call,-Lil C greeted him and went straight to the point.

"Would you mind taking a look at some cars (dope) anytime soon?" He asked. *"Of course not, "*Rob replied, showing his interest and availability.   The two planned a quick meetup. It had always been like that;

Lil C would call Rob and show him the stuff, and Rob would bid and end up buying almost every time. Likewise, when the two met at the table this time, Rob took a moment to inspect and analyze the bricks.

"I want to buy all six for 160," He offered the best price he could.

The bricks worthed 180 thousand dollars. '*160 isn't that bad.*' Lil C thought and almost agreed since he knew selling it to anyone else in the market might be less profitable and would be riskier. But he had to ask the boys first, as they were working as a team and had decided it to be 180.

"I would love to sell it to you at the moment, but for the price you've offered, I need to discuss it with fellows." Lil C requested some time from Rob, *"Give me a day, and I'll get back to you."*

"Sure, take your time."

The meeting ended, and the two went on their ways.

***

On his way back, Lil C summoned everyone immediately.

"101, ASAP." The text read.

As Lil-C entered the hideout, his guys, who had already reached the honeycomb hideout, bombarded him with questions. *"What's going on? Why have you called us all here again? Haven't we shared the profit already?"*

"Yes, we already did, but there is a thing you need to know."

Lil-C then disclosed the buyer's offer to buy all six for 160. Even though the offered amount was 5-10 percent less than the actual value, each of them agreed to the offer, except Toyz. He wasn't ready to settle for any less than the original.

The rest just wanted to get rid of the bricks, so they did not think twice and agreed. But unlike them, when Lil-C revealed the bid, Toyz vetoed it.

"Fuck, no. This isn't for any good." He interjected. *"How can we settle for twenty less? This isn't twenty bucks. We are losing twenty thousand straight,"* he emphasized.

"We should look for another buyer," Toyz suggested.

"I guess this is fair because I believe no one would offer us a penny more, and since it is a whole lot of money so we better rely on someone trustworthy," Lil C reasoned his argument.

Lil-C's point was valid, but Toyz was not ready to admit it. He insisted Lil C demands more, *"it should be 180 thousand. Only then will I sell mine, as you assholes are already giving me less."*

On Toyz's insistence, Lil C spoke to Rob. But as he did not agree, nor did Toyz, Lil C locked the deal to sell five bricks instead of six for 130 thousand dollars. The two decided to meet again at a bar around the corner.

In the evening, Lil C and Rob sat face to face. Lil C handed over the five bricks and got a bag of 130 thousand dollars in return. Once the deal was over, the two continued sitting at the bar. They talked about an old Mexican friend who moved weight-and had just finished a bid −serving federal time in the penitentiary.

Rob had invited his niece Jess to join him afterward. So, he intentionally sat a little longer with Lil C while awaiting her response. The conversation first mentioned her, only for her to become the next topic. He inquired Lil C about Jess.

"I hadn't seen her for a month. Do you know what's keeping her busy nowadays?" Rob asked casually.

"Yeah, selling houses has been keeping her busy lately. She is trying to see if she can take-some time off to accommodate in Mexico."

'What? Selling houses?' Rob had sensed something was wrong. His face wore a weird impression, and he somehow covered it, saying, *"oh, okay."* Lil C, being an active minder, had registered the priceless look on Rob's face. And as his mind coalited words to phrase the inquiry, the phone on the table rang and diverted

his attention. He had a quick glance at the caller's ID. *Jess calling...* He picked up the phone playing super cautiously. *"Is everything okay?"* He asked immediately after answering the call.

She responded yes, he put her on hold, *"Give me a moment, please,"* and muted the call.

-Lil C then turned to Rob and said goodbye to him. As he parted ways with Jess's uncle, he resumed the conversation on the phone.

On the other side of the phone, Jess complained about reaching him a day before to no avail. *"I came to see you a day before, but you weren't at home, I guess."*

"Oh, yeah. I am really sorry. I was out gambling and stuff." Alex apologized regretfully.

"Oh, okay," she responded.

-Alex adjusted himself behind the wheel, asking Jess, *"So, have you decided about the trip yet?"*

"Yes. I believe that's exactly what I need – a weekend free of work stress."

Chapter 7: "Key Evidence"

Jess and Alex wandered in the busy streets of Mexico. They chattered, jumping from one thing and another. A familiar sound of music reached their ears. Alex turned his head to figure out where it was coming from – the second floor of an unknown apartment. He began jerking his neck in rhythm, syncing with the lyrics.

As Alex's lips traced the words silently, Jess noticed the charisma. *"You like this?"* She asked in excitement, with her eyes looking deep inside his.

"Yeah, I do," Alex replied, reaching for her hand.

Her arms around her waist unfolded, and she gave in. Alex smiled at her holding her fingers from the upper end. He took a few steps back, moving her arm up, inducing her to whirl around. Jess chuckled, and at every round, she exchanged eyes with him.

Jess took a deep breath; she felt incredible. The essence of having him closer made her cheeks blush. She, once again, turned around to dance on the street with him, *"eehh,"* her body hit the bed.

Her eyes flashed open in response, leaving her surprised. *"Wait, what?"* She jumped up, sitting straight on the bed, *"Wasn't in Mexico?"* Jess's gaze toured across the room for Alex, *"Where is Alex?"*

The familiar interior and everything around soon made her realize she was at home. *"Means it was all a dream?"* She thought, *"Ughh!"*

Jess put her hands up on her head and closed her eyes for a moment again, *"wish we could live in dreams for as long as we want."*

***

Jess was now awake completely. She got out of bed, and after doing the bathing rituals, she moved into the kitchen. Hungry? Yes, that was exactly what she felt at the moment.

It was 6:45 in the morning. *"Woah, right on schedule!"* Jess remarked herself, as she would usually wake up an hour late, knowing that she would have to reach the office by 9.

Some bread, eggs, milk, and coffee – that's all for breakfast. As Jess brewed a cup of hot coffee, she switched on the LED using the remote. Although women usually don't prefer for news to be the first thing in the morning, being a cop, Jess's mornings were all about it. She didn't even need to switch the channel since the screen turned on featuring Live CBC News.

While Jess was pouring her coffee into the mug, the alert sound of *'breaking news'* diverted her attention to the TV. The image of three masked men that she had encountered a few months ago covered the whole screen. She had recognized the appearance at first sight, and now she was looking for something more than that. Leaving her breakfast then and there, Jess rushed out into the lounge. She was desperate to know what had happened, and it bothered her so much that she couldn't sit down. She stood before the huge screen and raised the volume.

"Three masked robbers are reported to invade another house." The reporter read through the headline visible on the screen.

"This is not the first time they have walked inside a home and ran out with everything; the robbers attempted a similar kind of robbery four months ago in New York."

Jess stood in awe with her eyes wide open. She seemed to be in disbelief, *"How could they do this again?"*

She hit one hand on another, *"Shit, shit!"*

"This wouldn't have happened if I had caught that juvenile," She cussed herself, recalling the moment when she had missed Toyz.

"Damn!" Jess didn't care to listen to any more of the details. She turned away from the TV and hurried back into the room. Her phone had already begun to ring consistently. As she slid her shirt off, she held the cell phone to her ear. *"Yes, Sir! I will be there in 10,"* she said and threw her phone on the bed.

***

The NYPD Headquarters was in chaos. Officers hassled here and there with their coffees and files in hand. The moment Jess arrived, she clocked in and hurried straight into the conference room.

The Chief of the New York Police Department had called an urgent meeting. All the officials, including Jess, had made it there on time. The meeting was to devise an action plan to catch the culprits, the team of three masked robbers. The debates and discussions continued for an hour. And with that, the meeting was adjourned at ten, only to rebegin a few hours later. The Head of the Department formulated a team of five leading officers. The newly formed team was to investigate the robbery, which must have spread to the nooks and corners of New York, or in fact, far away by then.

The city dwellers were all terrified. Political leaders, celebrities, and even local people questioned NYPD. The Mexican couple, targeted by the robbers, almost losing all they had, gave interviews to the media stations. The man criticized NYPD for its failure to not rescue them on time. *"The robbers could have been caught only if the police had arrived on time,"* he said in one of his many statements.

With every member busy analyzing the situation, Jess began her research. She surveyed all the news that had been reported regarding the robbers and was amazed to find out that there had been 17 of them in total. At around 1 PM, Jess had another meeting. This time, she didn't have to sit back, discuss, and argue. She would rather have to get into action and work with her team members. Jess stood around the circular table, dressed in fitted jeans and a white button-down shirt with a checked blazer on top. With a marker in hand and her head down on paper, she had just pointed out a different angle to the story.

"We need to think with a criminal mindset. What would be our next move? Because that's the only way we can get a step ahead to catch them," she remarked and continued, *"so the sooner we get it in our heads and start, the better it'd be!"*

The officials nodded, saying *"yes"* in unison, and before they dispersed out onto their desks, the cell phone placed on the central table buzzed.

-Alex *is calling...* Her eyes read, but she ignored it and said, *"Let's get going."*

***

"Where were you? Why didn't you pick up my call this morning?" Alex sounded concerned. *"I have been trying to reach out to you the whole day. I was worried."*

Jess, on the other hand, had been on her toes all day. *"Sorry, I was a bit busy at work today!"* She avoided getting into the details.

"Oh!" He snuffed as if her reply had wiped off all his doubts in one go. *"You could have informed me, but you didn't even pick up. That's not like you."* "Aww, Alex," Jess adored him caring for her. *"I know I needed to call back, but I really didn't find any time to. You know how things go hustling and bustling to places all day."* She made an excuse

"It's cool."

Jess had somehow calmed down Alex. She relied on her real estate job, which was only to keep her identity hidden as a cop, of course, and convinced him of how busy she had been traveling and visiting places.

"I'm so tired and have just reached home," Jess said, laying back on the couch in the lounge. *"What about you? How's your day, though?"*

"Good, I guess. I was just missing you," he added in a flirtatious tone.

Although Jess was talking to Alex, her mind was stuck on the facts about her case.

The NYPD police officers, who had been to the targeted house last night, had revealed the evidence – a piece of rope, that they found in the house in their search after the robbery. *"Jess,"* Alex called her name, *"you there?"* Her thought broke, and she responded, *"Yes, yes, what did you say?"* *"Nothing as such,"* Alex could sense Jess's mind was somewhere else, *"What's up?"* He asked to get more into her head to see what she was thinking about. *"Watching the news,"* she retorted without taking a second. *"News?"* He doubted if a woman like Jess could ever be interested in news.

"Yeah, what's wrong with that?" She asked, and before he said a word, she continued, *"Haven't you heard about the robbery today?"*

"No, not much," He pretended he was ignorant.

"Ah!" She sighed. *"Don't tell me you don't know about the masked robbers,"* her voice grew intense, *"they had been all over the news since they stole from the bachelors in main NY city,"*

"Oh, the one who ran off last time," He smirked.

-Alex's taunt triggered Jess's true instinct as a cop. *"Well, they won't be able to get away this time,"* she said in confidence.

"What?" He asked abruptly. *"I mean, how do you know that?"*

"This is what the news has stated because evidence has consistently been left behind." Jess put it on the authorities to cover for herself.

"Common sense! – the evidence will be fingerprinted, and that alone would be enough to reveal their identity!" she said, leaving Alex more inquisitive than ever before.

But on the other hand, Jess was bound to reveal minimal to none because of two major reasons; one, that she wasn't allowed to discuss the case as an official, and secondly, she had lied to Alex about her profession and now, she had no option except to keep lying to ensure she didn't break her cover.

Alex stood on the deserted street corner, his heart racing as he stealthy slid a sleek burner phone from his pockets. With fingers trembling in anticipation, he deftly tapped out a message, with his mind focused on the urgency of the situation.

"Meeting, URGENT," he typed, the words flashing across the screen in a blur of black and white. A surge of relief washed over him as the signal appeared-that his message had been delivered.

"Alex," Jess was still on the call. She called him by his name again, " Alex ...," until he responded.

"Hm," He hummed, sliding the burner back in his pockets.

Jess inquired if he was up to something besides her. Alex hesitated for a moment, unsure of how to respond. But he knew that Jess was sharp and that she would sense any hesitation in his voice.

So he quickly came up with a plausible excuse. *"No, not at all,"* he replied, his tone even. *"Just feeling a bit dizzy, that's all."* Jess seemed to accept his explanation. And Alex breathed a sigh of relief. But he knew that he couldn't let his guard down, not with so much at stake. So, he quickly changed the subject, asking, "What are you planning to do this weekend?"

Her mind raced as she tried to come up with a suitable response. She wanted to tell Alex about the robbery investigation she was leading, about how she was hot on the trail of the masked robbers. But she knew that she couldn't risk raising his suspicions. So she played it safe, replying with a noncommittal.

"Nothing special, I guess."

"Why don't we head to Mexico this weekend?" he suggested, his voice eager. *"I need to get there to see an old friend about work, buying and selling cars, you know."* He explained, offering, *"Why don't you join?"*

Jess was torn between her duty and her desire to spend time with Alex. She knew that she had to continue her investigation, but she also didn't want to arouse Alex's suspicions.

"Sure," she said, her voice brightening. *"But I'll have to get back by Monday morning then."*

"No problem," Alex understood, *"We can make it short and fun."*

Jess seemed to like the idea. She was already looking forward to the trip and had made the arrangements already.

But at the same time, she knew that the next few days were going to be tough. She would have to manage both her personal and professional responsibilities, all while keeping Alex in the dark.

It was a delicate balance, and Jess was determined to pull it off.

***

Meeting, URGENT.

JB and Toyz, each doing their own thing at different places, read the text. The alert had put them in a frantic state, wondering what was wrong. As each of them rushed toward the hideout, they had a clue. They were aware of the mistake they had made, leaving a piece of rope behind, yet the anticipation killed them until they reached.

-Lil C was calm and collected. His mind focused on the task at hand – to alert JB and Toyz. He briefly explained to JB and Toyz about the police's approach to the case. They discussed how it was convenient for NYPD to identify them through the evidence and talked about ways to avoid leaving their fingerprints anywhere. In the end, Lil C said, *"I'm leaving tonight,"* as they already knew what it meant – for Lil C to make a deal and traffic the dope. So, with no explanation needed, he informed them and advised them to be watchful. *"You two better be careful and watch out for yourselves."*

Chapter 8 "The Transport"

Jess, adorned in her relaxed denim and shirt combo, had eagerly prepared for this moment. Upon receiving Alex's text, *"I'm downstairs,"* she promptly descended to the vehicle. The two of them, in a frenzy to catch their flight, hastily embarked on their journey.

As they soared through the clouds, time seemed to be in warp speed. It was their first shared experience on a plane, as in relation, or perhaps something more, if fate permitted.

Jess sat in her seat, reclining it to a semi-horizontal position. She savored the sensation of her spine resting properly supported as she began to clear her mind.

With eyes shut, Jess took a deep breath and sighed in relief. Despite the criminal investigation - the culprits, the news coverage, the victims - being the primary focus of her thoughts, she was still able to find solace. A temporary escape from her mundane day job as a cop provided her with a momentary reprieve from the hustle and bustle of everyday life.

The flight, lasting five hours, could have left anyone tired. Yet, as the plane landed and the two disembarked, she felt refreshed. Her brief nap had reinvigorated her energy. And the fact that she was officially off-duty, even if only for two days, brought a renewed sense of purpose and vitality to her psyche. Jess was ready to jettison any chaotic or cluttered thoughts from her mind and enjoy the next couple of days with her companion, Alex.

Jess's heart skipped a beat as the crimson red Mercedes, a luxurious ride surely arranged by Alex, pulled up to the airport to whisk them away. She sat beside in the plush backseat. Her eyes feasted on the panoramic view outside, the wind teasing her hair, the sweet scent of adventure filling her senses, making Jess feel lively.

The ride took a little over ten minutes, and Jess remained clueless about their destination until the car pulled up at a magnificent building - The Palace Hotel. As they stopped, *"Finally,"* Jess exhaled as her eyes shining with anticipation met Alex. He had outdone it again, arranged everything with such meticulous attention to detail that it felt like he owned the city.

Alex asked Jess to wait for a moment while he went to grab the room keys. As she stood in the lobby, her eagle eyes scanned every detail, from the opulent decor to the fine art adorning the walls. Suddenly, Alex's voice broke her reverie. *"Hey, girl, let's get to the room. You must be tired,"* he said, sparkling with excitement. She chuckled softly, *"Not really, but I would prefer some rest first."* Jess couldn't help but notice the irresistible charm Alex was exhibiting. She felt an undeniable spark between them, one that had been ignited before the trip had even begun. As they entered the room, Jess's senses were bombarded with surprises. The room was adorned with stunning flowers and chilled champagne, a testament to Alex's thoughtfulness and romantic nature. Jess couldn't contain her excitement as she got on the bed, exclaiming, *"What a good day!"*

-Alex's voice cut through her thoughts, *"Ah! You like it?"*

Jess couldn't help but smile, her heart brimming with joy. *"Of course,"* she said, filled with happiness.

***

Jess woke up from a refreshing nap at around 4 o'clock in the afternoon. Alex had an important meeting to attend, so Jess decided to indulge in some solo swimming. She slipped into a chic black bikini that peeked out from under a flowing, knee-length dress, the fabric billowing in the warm breeze.

Using the lift, Jess descended to the ground floor. Her excitement mounted with every step. She strolled down the corridor, her senses alive to the sights and sounds around her, eager to dip into the cool, inviting waters of the pool.

As she made her way through the lobby, Jess didn't catch sight of Alex conversing with a man, too busy enjoying being on a break from her cop duties.

On the other hand, Miguel greeted Alex warmly, shaking his hand and embracing him with a grin. They had an air of familiarity between them. "Happy to see you home, man; told you I would come to see you when you got out," Alex said, his voice tinged with excitement.

-Alex responded with a chuckle, clearly pleased to be in his company.

"I never thought you would be waiting. I'm surprised," Miguel said teasingly. Alex looked at him, laughing at his antics. He was still the same.

They caught up more on the lost time, getting distracted as they talked about everything. As they grew aware of time, they realized they needed to make the discussion quick.

"*Let's discuss how the dope will be transported,*" the guy continued, his tone confident.

"The drug will be transported in a flatbed truck that carries cars. In this situation, we will fill the cars' engines with the substances."

-Alex looked at him intently, listening to his every word. "I have a connection with a US national. Pipelines of customers across the border. He'll catch up with the driver, swap the keys, and continue with the journey where the first one left off." They looked around to make sure nobody was eavesdropping. Making sure the coast was clear, the guy started to explain again. "As you and your group have the dope, you need to line up the smuggling in Mexico. You'll need around a week to make the arrangements. Get two flatbed trucks, estimating the weight of the substances around eight kilos. Compress the powdered drug within the pistons and fill it in the motor-holes of the cars. And your job is done."

Well, as the two discussed the plan, Alex cautioned him about certain things he knew well. In the end, as the guy stood up to leave, Jess was out of the pool.

Seeing her coming along the lobby, Alex quickly winded up. He said goodbye, trying his best to avoid interaction with Jess. Yet, as he shook hands and turned to leave, Jess met eyes with the guy who started walking towards the door.

"Give me a week, and we'll be on board," Alex said to the guy quietly before jogging back to her.

"What was that all about?" She asked inquisitively.

-Alex smiled, taking her hand in his. *"Just a little business deal, my love,"* he said, pulling her close. *"Nothing for you to worry about."*

He suppressed his sigh, *"Damn, you look sexy,"* Alex commented on brushing the air, which caused suspicion off them.

"It's your eyes, I guess," she responded, asking, *"Done with work?"*

"Yes," Alex replied as the two walked to their floor.

With that, the two headed back to their hotel room hotel. Their hearts were still racing from the excitement of the day. For Alex, it was just another successful transaction in a long line of deals that had made him one of the most notorious smugglers in the business. And for Jess, it was an adventure that she would never forget, a glimpse into the carefree, loving world that she could only imagine in her dreams a few months ago.

***

With Jess adoring Alex's minute gestures – from smiles to gentle touches, they both got ready to head out to witness the beauty of Mexico.

Jess wore a satin bodycon, navy blue in color. She had a silver necklace and a pair of earrings on as accessories.

As she stepped out of the restroom, with her hair styled back and her red lipstick, Alex was captivated by her elegance. He inched closer, smelled her neck, and asked, *"Ready? "As you can see,"* Jess flipped her hair strands and moved-towards-the door. The vibrant colors of the Mexican streets were filled with the rhythmic beats of music and a fusion of aromas from street vendors selling their tantalizing food. Alex and Jess walked hand in hand, lost in their own world, soaking in the warmth of the evening sun.

As they arrived at the restaurant, the charming ambiance with soft, warm lighting and tasteful décor welcomed them.

They were escorted to a cozy table by the window overlooking the enchanting cityscape. The menu offered a plethora of exquisite dishes, each sounding more delectable than the other.

-Alex and Jess indulged in a culinary feast, savoring every bite and relishing the experience.

The flavors exploded in their mouths, and their taste buds danced with delight. The night seemed magical, with the stars twinkling above and the city alive with a festive spirit.

As they finished their meal, Alex leaned over and whispered in Jess's ear, *"You look stunning tonight, my love."* Jess blushed, and her eyes sparkled with happiness. They paid the bill and stepped out onto the street, taking a leisurely stroll back to their hotel.

The cool breeze caressed their faces as they walked hand in hand, enjoying each other's company. They gazed at the starry sky, feeling grateful for this moment and for each other. As they reached their room, they embraced, and Jess said, *"Tonight was perfect."*-Alex smiled and replied, *"It was, yet it's only the beginning."* They kissed and melted into each other's arms, exploring the next level of their intimate connection.

Chapter 9: Early Bird Gets the Worm

As he keyed the ignition mindlessly and started the engine with his right hand, he sent a text from the other. It was a moderate day, not too hot, not too cold, yet Lil C could feel the sweat under his palms. It was the day of the shipment, and all things had to be carried out in order to keep a low profile.

Mandatory meeting at 7 a.m. The Hideout.

As JB reached their destination, he spotted Lil C gathering tools with his back to him. "Get these tools with me." He spoke without facing him, stacking them near the back of the truck. "They're in the form of compressed powder between the engines. You will need to take the engines apart to get them out."

"Leave this to me, Lil C." Lil C gave JB a nod. "Make sure not even a bit of the powder is left behind, and the engines are assembled back properly."

"These cars come from Texas and Mexico, and they'll be put on my lot," Lil C continued.

As easy as it sounded, the process was not easy. It required wits and speed and needed careful supervision and precision to mask the underground activities and not appear suspicious.

"How many kilos does this truck have?" JB questioned. "Each kilo is 17500. There's 8 in total," Lil C responded, stepping back from the truck as JB did his job. He started to disassemble the engines, the clank of metal filling the air as the powder slowly started to come into view. "By the way, heard from Toyz?" JB asked Lil C. Lil C nodded, dialing his numbers, which went straight to voicemail. Lil C immediately raised his brows, he went back to work and got a call back around 8:30 a.m. "Why aren't you here?" Lil C asked.

"Phone died. Had to wait until it could charge enough, so I just saw your message," Toyz replied.

Lil C sighed. "Get to the hideout as soon as possible. We need you here."

Upon arrival, Toyz got into an argument with JB over being late, which Lil C had to break up.

"Excuse me? Why do we have to pay $17,500 per kilo?" Toyz stepped forward, hands in his pockets. Lil C rolled his eyes, taking a deep breath. "You should be paying more than that. You are always doing fucked up shit, you act like a bitch."

Toyz had started to walk toward Lil C. Toyz was a difficult man. His patience dwindled significantly every time he was around him. "You only paid $10,500per kilo.

It is only fair for us so we all can eat," Toyz continued, his voice rising. Toyz had started to look around the room for any signs of agreement, as the boss remained neutral and silent. Lil C sighed. "I just think maybe you're overreacting a little." "Overreacting? This is not fair and square. Bring the prices down, or there will be no deal from me." Lil C clenched his fist as his ears turned red. Toyz was incredibly obnoxious, always trying to start an argument with anyone who breathed. But today, his patience was running even thinner.

"We should have left your ass a long time ago."

"My bad, it was my fucking mistake asking the boss to let you back in, you bitch," JB said.

Toyz fumed and charged toward JB; Lil C came in between them, casually standing as he pulled out a cigar. Toyz halted abruptly, staring at him with fear.

"Get your feet out of your ass; that's what you need to do," Lil C said, lighting the cigar as he stood confidently. "Get a kilo each. Give Sharad and Terrel a brick a piece - 17500. For Toyz and JB, you get a kilo for the same price. No negotiation."

Toyz huffed as he looked away, running a hand through his hair. He had expected the price to go down by a few numbers.

Meanwhile, Lil C started pacing around as he sent a text to an unidentified number through WhatsApp that read "North Lot Ready." An instant response back was "BET." It was already understood that the pick-up would happen the next day, early morning.

Lil C stepped back into the room, looking at the men stuffing the powder into cereal boxes. They were stealthy and had an idea of what they were doing.

"Find a storage space we can put this money in, as well as a safe house for the next shipment."

"The next shipment will be bigger.."

Lil C understood the risks of using the same place.

Make sure you assemble the engines back properly. Be careful."

The sun had barely risen as birds chirped in the background. The weather was pleasant during the mornings, but the heat became unbearable by noon. Lil C pulled up to the dealership, stepping into the premises. Clean and proper, no person in their right mind could guess what went on behind the scenes. To a normal eye, it would look like a clean, legal car dealership.

The men should be here in a few minutes. His plan had to go smoothly, and he had to make them think the drugs were not being stored there, although they had been here all along.

Time goes by, and a car pulls up into the shades in front of the dealership. The men got out, and Lil C stepped out just in time to greet them. "The packages are not here yet. Come back in 30 minutes, and I'll be here with them."

The men looked at each other before getting into their cars, watching as Lil C pulled away in his own car. After driving around a bit, he pulled back to the dealership after making sure they had left.

He got the drugs ready in their packaging, making sure all was done under the short time crunch. As time zoomed by, the men came back, under the impression Lil C had arrived back with the drugs. They received the packages from him, made the purchase, and left swiftly.

Chapter 10: The Investigation

Jess entered the restaurant, her heart pounding with a mix of exhilaration and eager anticipation. The prospect of meeting her long-lost friend Kim, whom she hadn't seen or spoken to in several years, filled her with excitement. Their bond had lasted for over a decade, and Jess knew without a doubt that Kim would always be there for her.

Scanning the bustling establishment, her eyes finally settled on Kim, comfortably seated at a corner table, engrossed in her phone. With an exuberant smile illuminating her face, Jess approached Kim and embraced her with in a warm, affectionate hug. "Hey, stranger!" Jess exclaimed joyfully.

Kim looked up. "Hey, Jess! Long time no see, stranger!" Their hug lasted a while as they relished in the last few seconds of the long-forgotten embrace. The two settled into their seats, looked over the menu, and promptly placed their drink and food orders. To Jess' relief, there was no lingering awkwardness or hesitance between the two.

They had picked up where they left off, and Jess felt grateful for that. It was good to have her friend back. Initially, their conversation flowed at a leisurely pace, but before long, the two friends were engrossed in animated chatter, eagerly catching up on all the latest happenings and anecdotes from their respective lives. As they shared pictures of their lives, they discussed different milestones they had achieved, from first apartments to jobs to family. In the midst of their lively exchange, Jess retrieved her phone and proudly presented a series of pictures of her new boyfriend.

A radiant glow adorned her face as she looked at Kim. "He's absolutely adorable, don't you think?" Kim leaned in, studying the images closely, and arched an eyebrow playfully.

"Well, he's certainly cute, but have you done any background checks on him?" A cloud of confusion descended upon Jess as she sought clarification.

"Background checks? What do you mean?" Kim leaned forward, her expression growing earnest. Jess had always been a little naïve, but Kim was always the rational one of the two. "The world can be a dangerous place, and it's essential to ensure you truly know who you're getting involved with." Jess nodded with a flicker of concern now presented within her.

A realization set deep within her as she listened to Kim's advice and realized that she was, in fact, saying the right thing. "You're right. I'll definitely look into that." The conversation shifted gears, turning towards Kim's own love life, or rather, the lack thereof. A twinkle of mischief appeared in Jess' eye as she looked at Kim, ready to interrogate her about everything. "I simply don't have the time for dating," she confided, her tone matter-of-fact. "Work keeps me far too occupied." Jess chuckled, affectionately acknowledging Kim's straightforward nature. "You're so refreshingly blunt, Kim. You're like the embodiment of candor, almost like a man." Kim joined in her friend's laughter, taking her remarks lightly.

They always had a sarcastic, joking banter, and that made their bond much more special and unique. "Perhaps I am. But hey, at least I'm always honest. Toast to us for all we have been through, with and without each other." Raising their glasses in a toast, they celebrated their enduring friendship and reminisced about the incredible journey they had shared so far.

"I'm so glad we met up again, Jess." Jess held Kim's hand as she looked at her endearingly. "I would not let that happen."

Returning to the topic of Jess' boyfriend, Kim inquired about his profession. Pride filled Jess' voice as she replied, "He actually owns a thriving car dealership." Impressed, Kim expressed her admiration. "Wow, that's fantastic! Remember when you didn't even know where your ex-boyfriend worked?" Jess lightly choked on her wine with laughter, her expressions scrunching in disbelief. "God, I can't believe I was that stupid before."

"Maybe you still are?" Kim playfully shrugged before digging back into her meal. Their conversation continued, intermingled with laughter and shared memories. Eventually, Jess asked Kim for a favor, requesting her assistance in running some checks on certain individuals. Kim reciprocated, inquiring about Rose, Jess' mother. Eagerly, Jess shared the good news. "She's doing incredibly well! She's found love again, and they're planning to relocate to Georgia." Kim's smile mirrored Jess' joy. "Rose is an extraordinary person. I'm genuinely thrilled to hear that."

Subsequently, Jess playfully hinted at Kim performing a background check on her boyfriend, prompting Kim to tease her about wedding bells. "I see you are already smitten. I like that. It looks cute on you. The look of love," Jess said as she playfully nudged her, chuckling as she declined the suggestion. "Tell me the name of the mom's boyfriend. I'll run his ass through a check since he's with the family."

Their conversation meandered toward Kim's uncle. "How's your uncle? I still remember when I represented him to save his ass from imprisonment." He still has not paid me my money. Jess sighed. "Still the same. He runs a fancy restaurant now,"- The two then continued their meal, promptly distracting themselves from a heavy conversation. This was supposed to be a lighthearted reunion, not a heavy one. The two continued catching up, lost in conversation, and made plans for what to do after dinner. However, their pleasant interlude was momentarily interrupted as Kim's phone chimed, demanding her attention. Apologetically, she excused herself, explaining the importance of the call. Before parting ways, Kim embraced Jess tightly. "Don't forget me, bitch! Let me know whenever you need help. Background checks or whatever. I'm always here for you, so let's keep in touch more from now on."

Jess gives her a light cheek kiss, patting her on the back to urge her to leave. It was an important call, and she could not let her friend miss it.

As she watched her dear friend depart, a profound sense of gratitude for their enduring friendship flooded her heart. She hoped they would meet up more often and be there for each other more through the joys and challenges.

***

Jess sat nervously on her couch, playing with her thumbs as she waited for Kim to arrive. It had been a week since their last conversation about her supposed Mr. Right. Jess had excitedly told Kim all about him. But now, she was filled with a sense of dread, wondering what information Kim had uncovered about him.

The doorbell rang, and Jess jumped up to answer it. Kim was standing there, looking both grim and triumphant. Jess ushered her into the living room, and they settled on the couches. "Well?" Jess asked, unable to wait any longer. Kim took a deep breath before launching into her findings. She had spent the week scouring the internet for any information on Jess's man, and what she had discovered was shocking.

"First of all," Kim began, "He's been in jail for drug conspiracy. He was released a few years ago, but still, it's not a great look." Jess's jaw dropped.

How had she never known any of this about him? She had thought he was a good guy, but this revelation had her questioning everything.

"And," Kim continued, "He's married. He has a whole wife." Jess felt her heart sink. Was their entire relationship built on lies? Kim pulled out her phone and showed Jess pictures of his wedding day, with him standing beside a beautiful woman in a white gown.

Jess felt like the rug had been pulled out from under her feet. She had invested so much of herself into this relationship, only to find out that it was nothing but a sham. Kim tried to offer words of comfort, telling Jess that she deserved someone who would be honest with her and treat her with respect.

But Jess couldn't help feeling hurt and betrayed. As Kim left, Jess was alone with her thoughts. She realized that she had been so desperate for love and companionship that she had been willing to overlook any warning signs.

The anger Jess had endured for a split second she knew that she needed to think things through before speaking with Alex. She drowned herself in her own tears until she had fallen asleep.

Chapter 11: Mission Impossible

Meeting at 6 am today. Have all gear ready. Lil C sends out a text in the group chat.

Once everyone had arrived at the location, Lil C sat at the head of the table, looking out at his team. He knew this next lick had to be perfect, and he wouldn't let Toyz's previous mistakes mess it up. This was a big opportunity for them and had to be executed with no mistakes.

"Alright, everyone, we know the drill," Lil C began, tapping his finger on the building blueprint. "We've got to hit this place fast. Toyz, I need you to be on point this time. No distractions, no mistakes." Toyz nodded, his eyes focused on the blueprint.

This was his chance to prove his point to both Lil C and JB that he was on top of his game. As they prepared their gear, Lil C emphasized the importance of the walkie-talkies and handcuffs. "No ropes this time, guys. We can't afford to leave any evidence behind. Toyz, make sure you have everything locked down. Everyone knows their positions. We need to go in and come out as quick as we can."

Before leaving the honeycomb, they proceeded to conduct an equipment check, ensuring they all had the guns, magazines, radio check, cuffs, and keys.

Driving a large SUV, a black suburban that Lil C had provided off his car lot from Mexico, they arrived at approximately 9:30. Parking the truck in the back of an abandoned building, it was only a few feet away from the place of the lick.

Around 10:00 am, one guard would come out back for a smoke break, and they knew how to catch him off guard.

Everyone exited the truck as Lil C goes to the guard to distract him.

"Morning, man. Care to spare a cigarette?" He asks nonchalantly. The guy nods, reaching for a cigarette in his pocket as JB and Toyz walk behind the guard quietly. Disarming, handcuffing, and placing a gun to his back, they walk the guard in first, utilizing him as a shield.

Toyz remained downstairs while Lil C and JB climbed the stairs, their eyes darting back and forth as they looked for the other guard. Once they spotted the guard, they crept up behind him and disarmed him without any problems.

As the employees broke into a frenzy, Toyz shut them down with authority, threatening them to ensure they did not interfere with the plan.

They all surrendered their phones hesitantly, hands shaky as they sat close to each other on the ground. Toyz filled the bag with the cellphones, tossing it to the side. He was supposed to have locked the door and collected all the phones from the employees. However, his focus shifted when he saw a woman frantically trying to dial a number on the phone.

He swiftly grabbed the phone and shoved it into the bag, hoping no one had noticed. But within minutes, the dispatcher from 911 was on the line, listening to everything happening inside the building. The dispatcher calls the cops, alerting them of the robbery in progress.

As Jess was on patrol in the area nearby, she received the robbery alert, and her heart dropped. She needed to get there as soon as possible. "I'm en route." She said as she got into the car, keying the ignition quickly.

Unaware of all that was happening, they all proceeded with the lick. Lil C kept a cool head and devised a plan. "We've got to move quickly. Everyone, stay calm and stay focused," he instructed. JB's voice crackled over the walkie-talkie. "Lil C, is everything okay on your end?" Lil C replied, "Yeah, we're good."

"There is a whole underground business operating here. The employees are aware of it." Lil C speaks, "They're all in on it." But as they made their way around the building, Toyz could hear a voice coming from the bag. He froze for a moment, realizing what had happened. As he clumsily rummaged through the bag, he grabbed the source of the sound. It was the woman's phone. The dispatcher from 911 had overheard everything, and Toyz's stomach dropped as he realized the gravity of the situation.

Beads of sweat dripped down Toyz's forehead as he realized he had to alert the team. "Lil C, we have a situation. An employee called 911."

"We've got to get out of here NOW." Lil C quickly took charge. "Toyz, grab the loot, and let's move."

Lil C scrambled to find a glimmer of hope in the form of a getaway, and after a few frantic moments of searching mindlessly, he found one. "The backdoor to the left. Everyone leave from here!"

"Is the route clear?" JB asked, looking over the area. Unaware of Jess' presence, Toyz answered. "The stairs are clear. You can come down." JB began down the stairs as the officer was coming at the same time. "Drop your gun." It was a female officer with sternness dripping from her voice. Just as JB raised his weapon, Jess shot him, backing out from the establishment and taking cover.

"I need backup. Copy." She looked towards the door, aiming in case someone barged out with a gun. Toyz ran towards JB as he approached the stairs. Toyz sprang into action and pulled JB towards the back door. "Come on! Move!" He winced in pain, clutching his foot. "She shot me. I can't move." Toyz analyzed his wound, realizing the bullet had struck one of his major arteries. Toyz applied pressure to his wound, picking him up and taking him out the back door as Lil C waited in the getaway.

"Lil C, we're in trouble. JB's been shot," Toyz gasped as he struggled to keep up. Lil C got out to, help Toyz get JB into the backseat. "Toyz, we need to get him to a hospital." JB was losing blood fast, and Toyz started to panic again.

Why did you lie about the area being clear? Where did she come from?" JB asked Toyz in a hoarse voice. "The door was supposed to be locked." Toyz replied, "I thought I locked the door because the woman with the cell phone distracted me by calling 911. She was my main focus."

"Lil C, we can't take him to the hospital here."

Everything had gone sideways and become a mission impossible because JB had been shot. Toyz hung his head in shame.

Meanwhile, the police arrived at the scene and quickly assessed the situation. Shots had been fired, and there was evidence of a robbery in progress. They entered the building cautiously, guns drawn. But as they made their way through the building, they realized the robbers had already escaped.

As they continued searching, they noticed the workers huddled in a corner, looking scared and confused. They quickly rounded them up, trying to get answers to what had happened.

Jess hung around, giving descriptions and assisting with assessing the scene. Realizing the blood pools and splatter would be a key factor in finding out who she had just shot; she instantly delivered the samples to the lab. Also, seeing how much blood had been lost, she knew the person would need to seek treatment quickly.

As they questioned the workers, they realized this was more than just a simple robbery. They found drug paraphernalia scattered around the building, and several workers had tell-tale signs of drug use.

It was clear that there was something deeper going on here. As the hours went by, the police continued their search, uncovering more and more evidence of illegal activity.

They found cash, drugs, and weapons hidden throughout the building, evidence of a criminal enterprise hiding in plain sight.

Eventually, all the workers were taken to the precinct and booked for working in such an establishment, whilst having full knowledge of the illegal activities that were occurring.

Chapter 12: Man at Large

Kim felt the weight of the world lift off her shoulders as she collapsed on her cream-colored couch. She wore her favorite black leggings and a grey oversized sweater as she enjoyed her day off from work. Kim had planned to catch up on some Netflix shows with a bowl of popcorn in hand. However, she couldn't resist turning on the news and seeing the latest events happening around the world.

She flicked through the channels aimlessly for a while and then suddenly stopped at a news channel. The breaking news stories that unfolded interested her. The reports ranged from political scandals to worldwide events, but nothing seemed too pressing or urgent.

The saltish popcorn urged her to drink water, so she went to the kitchen humming songs to herself, and the TV ran in the background.

Kim returned to the living room to the blaring news from her television, with the anchor's voice firm and urgent. Her eyes were glued to the screen, and her mind raced with thousands of apprehensions; she sat on the couch with her glass of water.

The news report left her worried because it was about the dangerous case Jess was working on. And the news report confirmed her fears. "Many employees and managers were arrested from the scene under the suspicion of multiple charges of illegal activities." The reporter continued. "The robbery suspect left blood at the crime scene, which made it easier for the authorities to recognize the suspect."

"The suspect, Johnny Blake, is still on the run after being involved in a string of crimes throughout the city," the anchor said. A male figure flashed on the screen, identified as Johnny Blake. "If you see the suspect or know his whereabouts, please contact 1-800-555-TIPS."

Kim felt a sharp pang of recognition flood through her. She racked her brain, recalling where she had seen him before. Was he someone she had represented in court? Without hesitation, Kim reached for her phone and dialed Jess's number. She needed to know if her friend knew the person she had shot.

Ring, ring, ring

"Hey, Jess. What are you up to?" Kim asks.

"Headed into the office to finish up my report from the shooting," Jess responds.

"Have you come across the news yet?" Kim abruptly questioned as her mind was clouded with worry. "What news? What are you talking about? I'm driving right now. I haven't come across any news yet.

Is everything okay?" "Drop by my house if you can, please. I'll tell you." Kim cut the call. Jess was anxious and had to stop by Kim's house immediately. As Jess arrived, Kim hugged her.

"Thank goodness you're here. My anxiety was killing me." Kim lightly massaged her chest, taking a long sigh.

"You had me on the edge of my seat the whole car ride. What is it?" Jess inquired, mind not paying attention to anything Kim was saying.

Kim took Jess' hand and dashed towards the television. They both sat on the couch. Together they watched the news report, both feeling a sense of dread as they gazed at the picture of Johnny Blake on the TV screen.

"Do you know him?" Kim asked, her voice shaking slightly.

Jess's eyes narrowed as she studied the man. "He looks familiar," she said slowly, "but I can't quite place him." Kim's concern deepened as Jess tried to recognize the man from the news. She knew that Jess's work often involved dangerous situations, but this felt different. The tension in the air hung thick between them, both feeling a sense of unease.

With her mind buzzing and her thoughts in chaos, she was determined to get to the bottom of who Johnny Blake was and any possible connection to her personal life. But the true danger of the situation was just beginning to unfold. Jess's heart pounded with fear and anticipation as she watched the television, her mind swirling with possibilities. The news report had identified Johnny Blake as the person she shot, but Jess knew him by his alias, JB.

"Do you remember?" Kim questioned. "No." She answered.

"Oh fuck, I do. This dude hangs out with Alex!" Jess thinks to herself, short of breath. "I've seen these two together."

Kim's eyes widened as she rubbed her temple with her other hand. The coincidences were too well-aligned for Alex not to be involved.

As the news report played out, Jess's phone began to ring. She saw Alex's name on the screen, and panic rose. The fact that he was calling after seeing the news report made her even more suspicious. Holding her phone with shaky hands, she picked up his call, taking a deep breath.

"Hey, what's up? Can I call you later? I'm in a meeting right now."

"Sure, we seriously need to talk." Alex responds.

"Okay, I'll call you as soon as I finish up. Talk to you soon." Jess sat back, leaning against the sofa as she rubbed her eyes. She tried to connect the dots between the flashing events before her. Her mind raced with potential explanations as she tried to determine why Alex had called her in such a hurry.

Jess's mind raced with thoughts of her uncle and Alex being so comfortable with the gentleman during the Mexico trip. She remembered their conversations and how he had always seemed to hold secrets back. And then there was the fact of his past incarceration for drug conspiracy.

As she sat there, Jess's fears grew stronger. "Could the man I had been seeing, Mr. Right, actually be Mr. Wrong?" or "Was he the person of interest in the crimes I was investigating?" The weight of everything unfolding before her was overwhelming, and she felt her chest getting heavier with panic.

And then there was the fact of her late menstrual cycle and the possibility of pregnancy. This piece of information was never disclosed to Kim.

The thought of having a child with someone she barely knew and could potentially be involved in such crimes made her contemplate life as a whole. Would I have to choose my career over love? What will the effects of having a new baby be on my career? Would I have a support system?" How would work-life balance work for me?" Do I truly want kids? What do I really know about this man and vice versa?

For a moment, Jess was lost in her thoughts, trying to decide what her next move should be. But she knew she couldn't just run away from the truth forever. She snapped out of her reverie with a deep breath and decided to face the unknown head-on.

She snapped out of it and then proceeded to leave. She rushed out, telling Kim she must leave because of work.

The unknown was killing her as she rushed out to her car. Before she could backout of the driveway she calls Alex phone.

Kim runs outside yelling Jess name to catch her with new information on Alex. She is in such a zone that she doesn't even see or hear.

Jess's heart raced as Alex's phone ringing, hoping beyond hope that he would answer.

After a few seconds, the phone rang twice before a woman's voice answered.

"Hello?" the woman on the other end of the line said. Jess's heart sank. This wasn't Alex's voice. She hesitated for a moment

before asking, "Who is this?" There was a brief silence on the other end of the line before the woman spoke again. "Who are you looking for?" she asked. Jess's mind raced as she tried to think of what to say. She knew she couldn't reveal much but needed to know who this woman was. "I'm looking for Alex," Jess said, shaking slightly "Who is this?" Jess asked, trying to keep her voice calm. There was a pause on the other end of the line Jess's heart sank as the woman hung up the phone.